We Can Help!

by G. P. Drummond

Illustrated by Janet Street

Editorial Offices: Glenview, Illinois • Parsippany, New Jersey • New York, New York
Sales Offices: Needham, Massachusetts • Duluth, Georgia • Glenview, Illinois
Coppell, Texas • Sacramento, California • Mesa, Arizona

Farmer Ed was sad.
"I must get my crops to market."
Crops are plants. Farmers sell them.
"But how?" he said.

The cow had a plan.
The horse had a plan.
The goat had a plan.
The duck had a plan, too.

They met in the barn.
"Here is how we can help,"
said the cow.

"We must use our heads," she said.
"Let us think about going to market."

"I can use my nose," said the cow.
"I can use my horns," said the goat.

"I can use my legs," said the horse.
"I can honk," said the duck.

They helped Farmer Ed go to market.
It was fun to help.